The Library of Living and Working in Colonial Times™

A Day in the Life of a Colonial Soldier

J. L. Branse

The Rosen Publishing Group's
PowerKids Press™
New York

For my father

Published in 2002 by The Rosen Publishing Group, Inc.
29 East 21st Street, New York, NY 10010

Copyright © 2002 by The Rosen Publishing Group, Inc.

First Edition

Book Design: Danielle Primiceri
Layout Design: Maria E. Melendez and Nick Sciacca
Project Editor: Frances E. Ruffin

Photo Credits: Cover and title page, American Soldier loading musket © North Wind Pictures; p. 4 (Daniel Webster Birthplace) © Lee Snider/CORBIS; p. 7 (Wolf and Montcalm) © Bettmann/CORBIS; p. 8 (Boston Tea Party) © Bettmann/CORBIS; p. 11 (Portrait of King George III) © Archivo Iconografico, S.A./CORBIS; p. 12 (British Soldiers marching) © Kelly-Mooney Photography/CORBIS; p. 15 (Rifles) © Kelly Harriger/CORBIS; p. 16 (MAPS.com/CORBIS); p. 19 (Minuteman statue at Lexington) © Kevin Fleming/CORBIS; p. 20 (Battle of Lexington) © Bettmann/CORBIS.

Branse, J.L., 1965–
   A day in the life of a colonial soldier / J.L. Branse. — 1st ed.   p. cm. — (The library of living and working in colonial times) Includes bibliographical references and index.   ISBN 0-8239-5819-1
   1. Lexington, Battle of, 1775—Juvenile literature. 2. Minutemen (Militia)—Massachusetts—Lexington—Juvenile literature. 3. Soldiers—Massachusetts—Lexington—History—18th century—Juvenile literature. 4. Massachusetts—Militia—History—18th century—Juvenile literature. 5. Massachusetts—History—Colonial period, ca. 1600–1775—Juvenile literature. 6. Massachusetts—History—Revolution, 1775–1783—Juvenile literature. 7. United States—History—Revolution, 1775–1783—Causes—Juvenile literature. [1. Lexington, Battle of, 1775. 2. Minutemen (Militia) 3. Soldiers—History—18th century. 4. Massachusetts—History—Colonial period, ca. 1600–1775. 5. Massachusetts—History—Revolution, 1775–1783. 6. United States—History—Revolution, 1775–1783—Causes.] I. Title. II. Series.
      E241.L6 L36 2002
      973.3'311—dc21   00-011635

Manufactured in the United States of America

Contents

1	A Family Farmer	5
2	British Law	6
3	Taxes and a Tea Party	9
4	An Angry King	10
5	Redcoats and Minutemen	13
6	Preparing for Battle	14
7	An Early Morning Signal	17
8	Waiting for the British	18
9	A Shot Is Fired	21
10	The Battle of Lexington	22
	Glossary	23
	Index	24
	Web Sites	24

A Family Farmer

Stephen Wells woke at sunrise on April 18, 1775. There were many chores to do on the small farm in Lexington, Massachusetts, where he lived with his wife, Hannah, and son Luke.

Stephen felt worried as he ate breakfast with Hannah and Luke. He had heard that a war might break out between the American **colonists** and the British who ruled them. Stephen was a soldier in a **militia**. Nearly every American **colony** had a group of soldiers who were trained to defend their colony against the British.

◀ *Most colonial farmhouses were made of logs. This one belonged to Daniel Webster, an Early American statesman.*

British Law

Like all colonists, Stephen Wells had to follow the laws set down by the British king, George III. Stephen's family always had been **loyal** to the king. Stephen's father, Henry, had even fought alongside the British in the French and Indian War. From 1754 to 1763, the British fought against the French and their Native American **allies** for North American territory. Although Stephen had missed his father during that time, he was proud that Henry Wells had fought for a good cause.

American colonists joined British soldiers to defeat France in the French and Indian War. With this victory, they ▶ gained large areas of territory in North America.

Taxes and a Tea Party

The war had cost England a lot of money. To raise more, the British made the colonists pay **taxes** on sugar, stamps, and tea from England. The colonists thought it was time for America to become independent from England. On the night of December 16, 1773, Samuel Adams, a colonial leader, and a group of men named the Sons of Liberty climbed aboard a British ship. They dumped 342 chests of British tea into Boston Harbor. This was to **protest** the tea tax. Later this event was called the Boston Tea Party.

◀ *Samuel Adams and his men were dressed as Mohawk Indians when they tossed British tea into Boston Harbor.*

An Angry King

By noon on April 18, 1775, Stephen and his son Luke had milked the cows and fed the hogs and chickens. Then they mended the fence around the garden that Hannah had kept for the family. Stephen did not want to leave his family alone to harvest their crops. He hoped the colonies could gain freedom from England without a war. He knew, however, that King George III of England was angry with protests against taxes. It was believed that Samuel Adams, a leader of the Boston Tea Party, was hiding in Lexington.

This is a portrait of King George III of England (1738–1820). ▶

Redcoats and Minutemen

Stephen Wells belonged to a militia called the Lexington minutemen. They were ready to fight at a minute's notice. The militia was made up of farmers and **tradesmen**. In 1775, there were fewer than 100 minutemen in Lexington. King George III had sent about 4,000 British soldiers to Boston. He also had closed Boston Harbor to all trade. He wanted the other colonies to see that they would be punished if they turned against him. This made colonists like Stephen even more certain that they needed freedom from England.

◀ British soldiers were called the Redcoats because they fought in uniforms with red coats. The minutemen were not professional soldiers like the British. They had no set uniform.

Preparing for Battle

After supper on April 18, 1775, Stephen Wells cleaned his **musket**. Stephen had no idea that about 700 British soldiers headed for Lexington were so close. The British had found out that the colonists had guns and **ammunition** stored in the nearby town of Concord, Massachusetts. They also knew that Samuel Adams and another colonial leader, named John Hancock, were hiding in Lexington. The colonists thought the British were coming to destroy their weapons. Word was sent that the British were on their way.

Items that the minutemen might have taken into battle included a musket, a powder horn (made from a cow's ▶ horn) for carrying gunpowder, a flask, and a lantern.

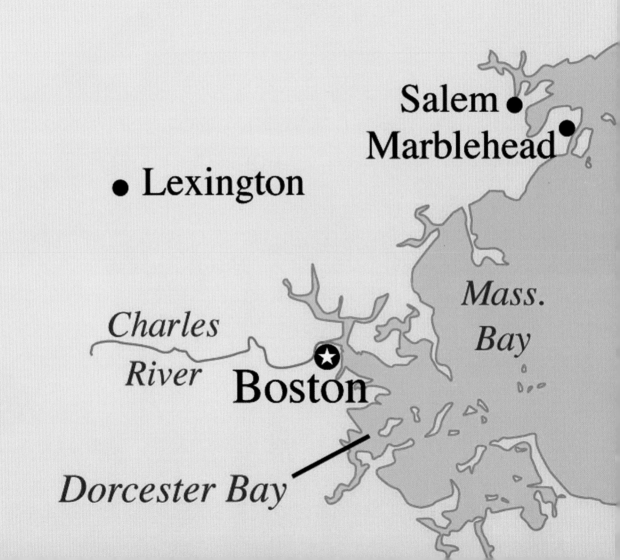

MASSACHUSETTS

Salem ●

Marblehead ●

● Lexington

Charles

River

Mass.

Bay

Boston ⭐

Dorcester Bay

An Early Morning Signal

A drumroll woke Stephen Wells at about one o'clock in the morning on April 19, 1775. This was the signal for the Lexington minutemen to meet on the town **common**. Stephen grabbed his musket and powder horn. He kissed Hannah and gave Luke a hug. On the way to town, Stephen met with his neighbor Joshua Moore. Both Stephen and Joshua were nervous and did not talk much. The British were practiced soldiers who had better guns than the minutemen. Stephen and the other minutemen would be facing a tough enemy.

◀ *Among the locations shown on the map of Massachusetts are the city of Boston and the town of Lexington.*

Waiting for the British

Stephen Wells, Joshua Moore, and the other minutemen gathered in Lexington to wait for the British to arrive. Their leader was Captain John Parker. Captain Parker ordered the minutemen to stand on the common in two rows. He told them to hold their guns but not to shoot unless the British shot at them. The minutemen waited for an hour, but the British were not close to Lexington. Captain Parker told the men to go home and listen again for the signal, the sound of the drummer.

The statue of Captain John Parker shows him holding his musket. He led the Lexington minutemen against the British on April 19, 1775. ▶

A Shot Is Fired

Three hours after leaving the common, Stephen Wells and the other minutemen heard another drumbeat. They returned to the common with their leader, Captain John Parker. When the British arrived in Lexington, they were surprised to see only 77 minutemen. They had been told that there would be 500 men. Major John Pitcairn, a British leader, told his soldiers to surround the minutemen and take away their weapons. He did not tell them to shoot. Suddenly Stephen heard a shot ring out. No one knows which side fired the shot.

◀ *A painting of the Battle of Lexington shows American minutemen and British soldiers.*

The Battle of Lexington

The minutemen did not put down their guns as the British ordered, but very few shot at the British. Only one British soldier was hurt. However, eight minutemen were killed and 10 were wounded. Even British Major John Pitcairn was ashamed of how his men had behaved. Stephen Wells never would forget the morning of April 19, 1775, and neither would any American. The Battle of Lexington lasted for only 15 minutes. It was the first battle in the **Revolutionary War**, America's war for independence.

Glossary

allies (A-lyz) Groups of people that agree to help another group of people.

ammunition (am-yuh-NIH-shun) Bullets, gunpowder, and other materials that can be exploded from weapons.

colonists (KAH-luh-nists) People who live in a colony.

colony (KAH-luh-nee) An area in a new country where a large group of people move.

common (KAH-mon) An open public area in a town or village.

loyal (LOY-ul) To be supportive of someone or take his or her side.

militia (muh-LIH-shuh) A group of people who are trained and ready to fight in an emergency.

musket (MUS-ket) A gun with a long barrel used for fighting.

protest (PROH-test) To act in a way that shows disagreement with something that has been done.

Revolutionary War (reh-vuh-LOO-shuh-nayr-ee WOR) The war that American colonists fought from 1775 to 1781 to win independence from England.

taxes (TAK-sez) Money that people give to government to help pay for public services.

tradesmen (TRAYDS-min) Shopkeepers as well as people who have special training and who work with their hands.

Index

A

Adams, Samuel, 9, 10, 14

B

Boston Tea Party, 9, 10

C

Captain John Parker, 18, 21
common, 17, 18, 21

Concord, Massachusetts, 14

G

King George III, 6, 10, 13

H

Hancock, John, 14

M

Major John Pitcairn, 21, 22
minutemen, 13, 17, 18, 21, 22

R

Revolutionary War, 22

W

Wells, Hannah, 5, 10, 17
Wells, Henry, 6
Wells, Luke, 5, 10, 17
Wells, Stephen, 5, 6, 10, 13, 14, 17, 18, 21

Web Sites:

http://hastings.ci.lexington.ma.us/Colonial/TheBattle/TheBattle.html
www.pbs.org/ktca/liberty/chronicle/lexington.html
www.wpi.edu/Academics/Depts/MilSci/BTSI/Lexcon